GW00707854

KNOT

alice maher draws from the collection of the hugh lane municipal gallery of modern art dublin

ALICE MAHER

This catalogue was published by the
Hugh Lane Municipal Gallery of Modern Art
Charlemont House, Parnell Square North, Dublin 1, Ireland
Tel: 353 1 874 1903 Fax: 353 1 872 2182 E-mail: hughlane@iol.ie

ISBN 1 901702 09 X

Photography by John Kellett
Designed and produced by Creative Inputs
Colour reproduction and printing by Nicholson & Bass
Catalogue co-ordination Christina Kennedy and Maime Winters

Cover: Sir John Everett Millais, *Two Figures on the Ground* (detail)
Alice Maher, *Coma Berenices* (detail)

This catalogue was produced with the financial assistance of
the patrons of the Friends of the Hugh Lane Gallery.

Corporate Patrons
Masterson and Associates; Office of Public Works
Patrons
David and Mary Casey, Mary and Anne Coolen, Brian Coyle, Una Crowley, Patrick Dawson, Marie Donnelly,
Michael Fitzgerald, Marianne Gunn O'Connor, Tony Hanahoe, Vincent Hendron, Josephine Kelliher,
Jerome and Deirdre Kennedy, Lainey Keogh, Padraig and Ann Lynch, Charles Masterson, Pat and Felicity McCartan,
Suzanne MacDougald, Paul McGowan, Frank and Susan McManus, Joan O'Connor, Gillian and Patrick O'Connor,
Mic O'Gorman, Patrick O'Reilly, Paul Quilligan, John and Catherine Reid, Anne Reihill, Norma Smurfit,
Alex and Maureen Spain, Ronald Tallon.

The practice of inviting an artist to reside temporarily in a museum or gallery is now a successful component of many institutions' annual programme. The resident artist is installed in a temporary studio which is open to the public, providing them with an insight into artists' creative procedures. Such interaction between audiences and artists is desirable.

On exploring novel ways of engaging art practice within the Gallery we concluded that not only is it desirable to invite an artist to work within a museum structure but we should also seek to present a continuum between past innovation and current creativity, and so Irish artist Alice Maher was invited to respond to our works on paper Collection and to curate the first major drawing exhibition from the permanent Collection.

The works on paper Collection in any Gallery is by its nature somewhat of a secret. Due to the fragility of their support these drawings cannot be publicly displayed for any great length of time and therefore are not as well known. But drawings play a valuable and significant role in the history of visual expression and are a central influence on many artists' work.

foreword

Alice Maher came to the Collection with a deep understanding of the drawing process, but with little or no knowledge of our holdings. Her informative, amusing introduction describes the process she adopted to select thirty-nine works for exhibition, ranging from the early nineteenth century French artist Camille Corot to the twentieth century artists Jack Butler Yeats and Paul Klee. The exhibition spans a period of over one hundred and fifty years during which time some of the most revolutionary practices occurred in the history of art.

It is true that not all the major players from this period are represented either in the Collection or in this exhibition but Alice Maher's selection is thoughtful and informed and includes many artists pioneering new areas of visual expression as well as those who performed a more traditional role of consolidating earlier innovation.

The works chosen provide visual parallel developments in art history of the late nineteenth and the first part of the twentieth century. Alice Maher's personal response to the selection resulted in four monumental charcoal drawings *Coma Berenices*. They were realised in direct response to two works in particular, *Sleep* by Keith Henderson and *Anima errante* by Paul Klee, two artists from opposite ends of art history.

Just as the works selected for exhibition thread their way through past achievements, the luxuriant Medusian coils in *Coma Berenices* are threaded into beautiful expressions of strength and femininity emerging out of contemporary experience.

The realisation of this exhibition could not have come about but for Alice Maher's complete commitment to the project. She was supported by our Head of Exhibitions, Christina Kennedy who with Alice brought the project to completion. My thanks also to Maime Winters, Liz Forster, Pat McBride, John Kellett and Creative Inputs.

Barbara Dawson
Director

The very best part of doing a drawing is not when you are finished, nor just before you start, but when you are right in the middle, like the centre around which a knot is tied. The reason for starting the drawing is in the past, and you haven't quite turned the corner towards its end. It is an incomparably tactile and timeless moment. It is not stand-back time, not proportion time, nor light and shade time. It is the time where the concept, content and activity are at seamless play. You are not 'lost' in your own occupation but surrounded by it, exquisitely busy, on an island between intellect and instinct. When I look at artists' drawings, I try to imagine where it was in that work that they got onto this 'island', when the fusion took place and the business kicked in.

I was curious when I first went upstairs to the attic of the Hugh Lane Municipal Gallery to snoop around in their collection of works on paper. There were hundreds of framed works, like ghosts leaning on each other. Some were stored in important cloth envelopes tied with ribbons, their titles embroidered on the outside. Others stood face to face, having seen no one for years. In the library there were drawers full of unframed works. These were all artists of whom I had only a small knowledge from art school; part of history yet peripheral now, many of them connected to Anglo-Irish society and to academicism, others to nineteenth century France.

KNOT

I thought, God, this isn't really the kind of work I like, it isn't my era, my area of interest. Should I look for an overall theme, some thesis on the image of the Irish peasant through the eyes of Anglo-Irish academic painters?

I kept going back and climbing the stairs looking for signs. The more I looked through the drawings in the quiet of the daylight high over Parnell Square, the more I let go the search for a unifying theme. In fact, the lack of unity became a liberating factor and I began to look in each work for that knot, that island, that personal moment with which I myself, or anyone who has ever made a drawing, could identify.

It is easy to spot that moment with an artist like Corot, where the soft rubbings of charcoal existed for some time not as foliage and fields, but as a meeting point for Corot's hand and mind. Millais's little figures in the wood seem to struggle with each other at the exact point where Millais got great joy from making shivery lines. Even Frederic Leighton's *Juggler* has a moment in it where it is not simply a study for some huge archaic scene. There is a personal moment there between himself and his ability.

After numerous visits to the attic I was able to pick thirty-nine works that have at their core the best moment of drawing, the one where the knot is just about to be tied around itself.

The era to which many of these works belong is now unfashionable. Artists such as Sargent, Augustus John, Osborne and Orpen were all welcomed into the 'society' of their day, but have come to represent a kind of dry vision which doesn't fit with the latter day image of a progressive and egalitarian twentieth century.

Hugh Lane and his friends believed that the art they were looking at was modern. Caught on the periphery of major art movements, they had sought to put together a modern collection for a modern city in what was fast changing into a modern state. Artists and collectors with whom they mixed had a huge effect on their taste and choices. Indeed a number of the drawings in the Collection were donated by the artists themselves, many of whom knew each other and worked together.

The teachers and pupils of the Slade School of Fine Art and the New English Art Club exerted great influence on the Lane circle. Paris and Rome operated as centres of excellence and study for many of the artists. The Collection evidences a broad interest in design and illustration, as well as a penchant for suppressed eroticism. Flirting with the exotic on far-flung travels was highly thought of, as was flirting with the Bohemian lifestyle. However, the emphasis in the collected works remains firmly on traditional values of drawing.

Almost all works are figurative, and many are allied to Classical themes. They are not disturbing pictures, either in content or execution. Many of the works are titled 'study', which sets them in an anonymous or minor key. The very ordinariness of the works gives one access to the extraordinary moments taking place at their core.

Studying what are considered minor artists is a way to understanding the complex history of the making of art. Corot and Puvis de Chavannes are two artists sitting quietly in this Collection who were predecessors to the great art movements of the twentieth century. And there are as many more here whose invisible influence has ebbed and flowed through the reservoir of contemporary thought and practice.

jean-baptiste camille corot

1796-1875

The landscapes of Corot seem to exist in the dimmest light, hovering somewhere before dawn or after dusk. This particular landscape drawing is a great example of an image of 'dissolve', that cinematic moment before or after a picture comes into focus. The feathery trees, the empty meadows, the whole composition hovers like a fog. It is suspended between focus and dispersion, between Classicism and Impressionism, between Arcadia and Ville-d'Avray.

It is difficult to place Corot within the history of art and I believe this is why he became important to a later generation of painters and was picked up by the avant-garde as an individualist. Corot was no slave to observed reality as the Impressionists were to become. His still and dream-like landscapes allowed room for the imagination of the viewer. This mysterious drawing could almost prefigure the work of Odilon Redon and the Symbolists.

Though never exhibited during his lifetime, the figure paintings of Corot were rediscovered in the twentieth century by Picasso and Braque. His simple statuesque characters painted in muted tones, often holding musical instruments, were a direct influence on Cubist imagery and colour.

The Seamstress, though not from the musician series, exudes a similar monumentality and strict harmony. Every detail of shape and texture is captured with frugal economy. Yet our senses are tuned to an overall mood by the almost palpable articulation of sound, the rustle of cloth, the hum of insects through the open window, the deft snip of the scissors.

landscape with figures

the seamstress

9

patrick tuohy

1894 - 1930

Tuohy poses this great colossus of the theatre above the viewer, like a statue on a pedestal. O'Casey's features, however, are so un-stone-like that they almost dissolve into transparent membrane. We are asked to look up to him and yet to see his humanity at the same time. So soft is the pencil work that the sitter's upper lip overhangs his lower with the succulence of a snail. This is no empty tribute to one of the great architects of Irish national identity, but a work of true identification of one artist for the other.

Tuohy's biographers always speak of discerning 'melancholy' in his work, but this may be with the hindsight of the young artist's death by suicide. I perceive his work differently, and see a radical humanism that was not simply allied to Irish nationalism. The influence of Zurbarán and Velazquez is clear in his paintings and his drawings seem to wilfully identify with the world of common experience. Given another twenty years output, Tuohy's personal brand of realism might have led to a different kind of 'national' art than the one we have inherited from artists such as Sean Keating.

portrait of sean o'casey

alphonse legros

1837 - 1911

If you dive below the vaporous surface of this silver point drawing, you will emerge in the atmosphere of the Renaissance. The monumental jowls of the older man and the imperious glance of the younger both mark these out as historic figures. But who are they? They are independent of each other, expressing power in youth and dignity in old age. They are not costumed or hatted; they loom out of their foggy ground like ships passing in time.

The 'lemoning' of the paper over the years has added to its mist-like surface. The dual influences of Dürer and Holbein are clear in the precise engraving and refined drawing. Legros taught etching at the Slade School of Fine Art towards the end of the nineteenth century. It is tempting to imagine that these are the very faces of the old masters so imitated at the time.

study of two heads

sir john everett millais

1829 - 1896

These three drawings show none of the incredible, almost hallucinogenic detail of the works of this well-known Pre-Raphaelite. He began with historical and biblical subjects and was famous for the exquisite detail of every blade of grass and freckle on skin in his complex compositions. His most famous painting was *Christ in the House of his Parents* which shocked Victorians with its super-real depiction of the Holy Family as common peasants. Much of his later work deteriorated into a kind of gloomy sentimentalism which became very popular with latter day greeting card manufacturers and can be found reproduced in gallery bookshops everywhere.

These drawings are so intimate, so simple, and so modest that it is difficult to connect them with the Millais of grand scale historic paintings. The small size of the works and the fact that the reverse of each is also drawn on, implies that they come directly from the artist's sketchpad.

The *Two Figures on the Ground* are struggling to become a drawing as much as they are struggling with each other, the agitated pencil lines mirroring the physical activity of the lovers. The drawing has an erotic charge that is more like private fantasy than study for a large composition. The *Two Figures in a Moonlit Wood* lean lovingly on each other to create a pyramid shape with their discarded mandolin at the base.

All these drawings are fresh and immediate, in marked contrast to the crafted detail which the Pre-Raphaelite Brotherhood espoused.

female figure

two figures on the ground

study for an illustration
to coleridge's *love* or
two figures in a moonlit wood

john singer sargent

1856 - 1925

The women in the portraits of Sargent generally display such bright-eyed and pinch-waisted blankness that it is hard to believe the artist did not hold his sitters in contempt. With a few skillful flourishes and highlights he captured society ladies in sumptuous settings, acting like the celebrity magazine editor of his day.

I picked this drawing of *Miss Anstruther-Thomson* because of her concentrated expression and because she is busy doing something other than staring knowingly at the viewer. She is leaning forward as she draws something, staring fixedly at her subject, seemingly unaware that Sargent is doing the same to her. Clementina Anstruther-Thomson was an artist herself and was interested in the philosophy and writing of her day. In 1897 she published jointly with Vernon Lee the intriguingly titled volume, 'Beauty and Ugliness and Other Studies in Psychological Aesthetics'.

Completed by Sargent in 1889, this is a simple drawing, fast and furious. His rush of light and shade and rapid outline capture the look of a woman who isn't simply making you aware of her social status. There is something awkward in the drawing of the left arm but his speed didn't allow time to repair it. Miss Anstruther-Thomson is dressed in the costume of a much earlier era, some research suggesting that the dress is a copy from the clothed figure in Titian's *Sacred and Profane Love*. This anomaly gives the portrait an interesting twist; the artist-model dressed in the guise of the artist's model and representing the 'profane' half of Titian's allegory. She has the passionate air of a Henry James character, clothed in the past yet straining toward the future. I wonder what her drawing was like and where it is now?

miss anstruther-thomson

17

augustus edwin john

1878 - 1961

Augustus John spent much of his time doing studies, mostly different versions of the same subject. Like film stills, these repeated images seem to capture every move of the subject in slow motion. He had a cartographer's precision when it came to line but this was often neutralised by a theatricality of pose. A figure lost in time, Augustus John never seemed to find his true subject and kept re-posing gypsies and other genre groupings, hoping to come up with historical compositions. He was friendly with Hugh Lane and travelled to Ireland to make studies of Galway peasants, all of whom look more like extras in an operetta than they do real people.

This drawing is called *Study of a Girl* but her pose and features all point to her being Dorelia, one of the two women in the life of Augustus John. We are given no hint, however, of the artist's involvement with the subject, who seems more like a model posing in ethnic costume for a life drawing class.

John's portrait of the literary historian *Joseph Hone* is a very different kind of drawing and suggests a real individual presence in the sitter. The brittle lines and wispish strokes of dry charcoal investigate age fearfully. The upward jerk of the head in motion is dynamic and shifts this drawing out of the realm of academic study.

study of a girl
(dorelia with a scarf)

18

joseph hone

simeon solomon

1840 - 1905

There are seven of this artists' works in the Collection. In style, Simeon Solomon falls somewhere between the Pre-Raphaelites and Aubrey Beardsley/Harry Clarke. His work is sentimental and self-conscious for the most part, but executed with such excess of delicacy and sweetness that it is dizzying to look at.

The Acolyte explores one of Solomon's favourite ritualistic themes of youth and old age. The companion piece shows pagan celebrants in willowy gowns. Executed in water colour, these works are almost overcome by the denseness of their own surfaces. Like over-ripe orchids, they exude a perfume that is at once oppressive and hypnotic.

Solomon was from a Jewish background and many of his early works explored Hebrew themes from the Talmud and Song of Songs. This all changed, however, under the influence of Frederic, Lord Leighton, when he turned to the more fashionable Classical and allegorical subjects.

Solomon had a fractious relationship with his family because of his homosexuality and the ambivalence of patrons toward his lifestyle, and perhaps his religion, meant that he never gained the popularity or fortune of his contemporaries. He was admired by Oscar Wilde, and like Wilde, was brought before the courts on moral corruption charges and ejected from the very society that had formerly adored him. Solomon ended his days in penury, sleeping rough and doing pavement drawings for a living. There are so many of his works in this Collection that one must assume he was greatly admired by Hugh Lane's circle to begin with. I wonder when the fall from grace occurred, or whether any of them passed Solomon on the streets of London as they went about the business of collecting art?

the greek festival

the acolyte

charles conder

1868 - 1909

Conder's works seem to always fall short of competence, yet they wink at you out of the Collection, like funny incidents. His Neo-Rococo style remains unconsolidated yet attractive in its carefree imagery of fêtes and masquerades. Conder's biographer wrote that the artist had 'the character of idleness'. He certainly does not seem to have produced much work. He was most famous for his exquisite paintings on fans, a practice also associated with Whistler.

The small drawing here is titled *Ladies by the Sea*. This is very close to sketchbook work; quick, intimate and on-the-spot. Two women are sliding down a sand dune, their clothes askew, their hair windblown. It is a funny, naughty picture, done in light-hearted haste. The other larger watercolour is called *The Bather* but could just as easily be another *Ladies by the Sea*. The setting is a Grecian idyll but it has none of the gravity of an archaic composition. The water colours have faded, leaving the blue ribbons of crayon to delineate dress. One woman is either dressing or undressing the other on a sunny terrace. This is more of a peep than a grand vista. Conder's lazy generalisation of hands and feet is a practice much deplored by life drawing teachers, and it is amusing to find it amongst all the worthy draughtsmen in the Collection of Hugh Lane.

the bather

ladies by the sea

sir william orpen

1878 - 1931

Orpen was a friend of Augustus John and we can see some similarity between the two in their dry style and elegant draughtsmanship. As with Augustus John, I have chosen two drawings from Orpen that express opposing sides of his work. The first is a formal study called *The Portuguese Woman*, the second an informal portrait of a close friend.

Orpen was a strict follower and teacher of academic principles, all of which are applied in *The Portuguese Woman*. The three quarter *contrapposto* position, partial nudity and graceful drapery, all add up to a faultless piece of detached observation. The model turns her head away in order to give us a better view of the superb drawing of her hair and neck. The antique earring and dark brows hint at racial exoticism. But this model could just as easily be a Galway woman posing in her embroidered shawl for the great society artist who, along with Augustus John, collected ethnic 'types' and genre scenes.

The drawing of *Hugh Lane Reading* is of an altogether different style and mood. Lane's pose, in a wicker chair with his back to the viewer, feet up on a stove or mantlepiece, is the opposite in every way of the formal portrait style associated with Orpen. Here artist and sitter share the same space as equals. The sitter is relaxed and unselfconscious, the artist's drawing style reflecting the same qualities. Orpen advised Lane in his art collecting and they often travelled together. In my imagination this scene is taken from one of those journeys. Both men are chatting and smoking in a hotel suite and Orpen just happens to have his sketchbook nearby. The open lines and lightness of touch show that Orpen was not entirely opposed to modernism in his own work.

the portuguese woman

hugh lane reading

frederic, lord leighton

1830 - 1896

Frederic, Lord Leighton became Director of the Royal Academy and was a lifelong exponent of its scrupulous dogma. From initial study to final glaze, Leighton brought each painting through all the prescribed stages. His obsession with surface finish and virtuoso drawing of drapery, ensured that his sentimental neo-Classical idylls became the perfect scenes for reproduction ad nauseam in calendar and greeting card form.

Most of his drawings were executed in black and white chalk on blue paper. *Study of a Nude Figure (Juggler)* shows clearly how Leighton 'built' a drawing from initial marks to an icy perfection. He relied heavily on contour to create form. The figure is frozen in action like a statue, awaiting her placement in a scene where each figure will have been formulated individually in just such a polished manner before being dressed and inserted into the overall composition. The pose is reminiscent of the mythological figures of Ingres. We know that Leighton was influenced by the French neo-Classicist, but the cool accuracy and marbled surface of Leighton's figures cannot compare with the voluptuous intensity of Ingres's odalisques.

study of nude figure (juggler)

jack butler yeats

The two works shown here are from a very early period in this well known Irish artist's long career. In the drawing of a horse and rider, we are not too sure which is the 'old slave' of the title. The horse is a monster with giant hind quarters and a tiny head. His rider casts a haggard glance at us over his shoulder, as both are about to move off in the direction of some wind blown tents. Detail is minimal yet precisely descriptive. Yeats manages to convey weather with a few vertical strokes and a low horizon. It is a workman-like, unpretentious drawing. The crisp black lines and economic use of colour ally this piece to poster design. Yeats's understanding of the physical workings of man and beast is faultless, and was to give way to a kind of psychic fusion of the two in his late paintings.

This wash drawing of *The Travelling Circus* is done on prepared board which means it was probably made outdoors and perhaps was even completed on the spot as the circus set up camp. Dusk is falling and the big top is lit from the inside like a beacon in the vast landscape. Veils of transparent colour reveal the magic hour of a summer evening when everything is a haze of blue, the days work is done and the long evening stretches ahead brimming with promise. A river of hats flows towards the majestic tent like penitents to a holy well.

In later years Yeats turned the landscape inside out, both literally and metaphorically. Form melted into the rivulets of paint that were to become his personal visual language as he imploded the mythic memories of place and people. In *The Travelling Circus*, form still holds, but just barely. We see the landscape as it is but there is something about to rupture its ordinariness. It is an awkward, beautiful picture, straddling the divide between illustration and expression.

the travelling circus

an old slave

wilhelmina geddes

1887 - 1955

The dark sweeping lines and simple forms of *Cinderella Dressing her Ugly Sister* anticipate Geddes's later move to working in stained glass. This watercolour and ink drawing even takes the tall format of a window. But the composition is more than a mere formalist device, as we are asked to look at this space as through a keyhole, into the timeless chamber of a well known tale. As with Yeats's early works, Geddes's drawings on paper prove to be much more than simply illustrative. The familiar is made strange by the power of its imagining.

There are 's' shapes everywhere; dresses, arms, curtains, ribbons; everything is an arabesque. One set of arms mirrors the gesture of the other. The acid yellow of the ugly sister's dress fills up the foreground like spilling poison, lit by the very mirror which deludes her. The harsh spotlight and shallow space add to the impression that we are voyeurs, sitting in the darkened theatre beyond the mirror, waiting for the familiar story to unfold.

In a strange visual twist to the tale, the vulnerable bare head of the ugly sister is dominated by a robust Cinderella who seems more intent on strangling than grooming her sibling. It is an unusual scene for the artist to choose to illustrate, showing a sense of humour that is both bright and deadly.

cinderella dressing her ugly sister

gerald brockhurst

Brockhurst was a north of England artist trained in the Arts and Crafts Movement, who lived in Ireland from 1914 to 1920. Many of his works of this period depict West of Ireland people. His portraits, though informed by traditional painting skills, have a cold realism that falls somewhere between Bronzino and Otto Dix. His dry quasi-Renaissance look became very popular with the monied classes, so much so that in the 30's, he moved permanently to Hollywood and became portraitist to film stars and their followers.

This drawing of a girl's head could belong to many different centuries. She has the athletic look of Picasso's model, Marie-Thérèse Walter, mixed with the lofty air of a Medici princess. A great column of a neck supports a head that is frank and informal. The hair is beautifully realised with the dense fringe giving way to heavy locks that are tied, Botticelli-like, at the nape of the neck. Despite the calmness of the pose, the eyes shine with an intense light that hints at something beyond the ordinary.

girl's head

george chinnery

1774 - 1852

Chinnery spent his lifetime recording scenes of the British colonies and the Far East, from Ireland to India, Macao to China. His sketches and paintings are like journalistic works, recording every particularity of the people; their costume, customs and occupations; their boats and houses, children and animals. In his two tiny drawings of cows, his pencil is both blunt and precise. He must have known cows very well to record their awkward squatness in such a practical manner. The marks which Chinnery makes are like a filigree of pencil twists and curls; a practiced and personal shorthand. His own abbreviated symbols for dates and places appear on the front of the drawings.

The small scale of the drawings does not denote intimacy of subject, however, as it does in the drawings of Millais. Here the animals and people are fixed in the middle distance, allowing us to observe them as we might watch a scene through binoculars. They remain the respected but curious residents of curious lands at the edge of a vast empire.

study of cattle

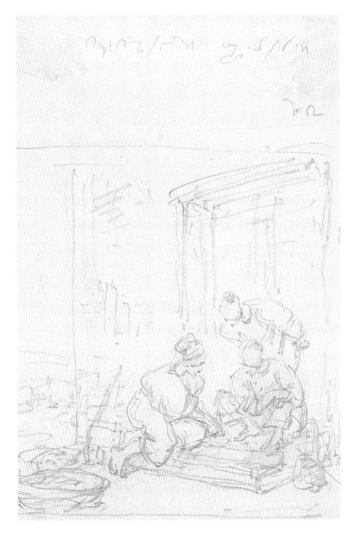

study of figures

william strang

1859 - 1921

William Strang became a pupil of Legros at the Slade School of Fine Art and specialised in etching. He made illustrations for *The Pilgrim's Progress* and *The Ancient Mariner*, and for ballads which he composed himself. *Study of a Head* shows the harsh line and high colouring of such popular narrative illustrations.

The adolescent heroine is drawn with the broad design of a comic book character. It is hard to believe that she does not have a name like Bunty or Judy. But for her old-fashioned dress and shining ringlets, this dour teenager could belong to any era. Her flushed cheeks and indulgent chin are very definitely articulated to create a singular personality, one who might feature in a weekly television drama or cartoon series. In her ribbons and high collar, this malcontent might be planning her next adventure.

Strang used the traditional illustrator's media of crayon and coloured pencil to describe this character who is much more than a caricature.

study of a head

charles françois daubigny

1817 - 1878

The tomb of Rousseau is the subject of this drawing, though it might just as easily be entitled 'A Gust of Wind.' The island tomb of the famous French man is tiny amidst the watery stretches of rush and weed and windblown trees.

Daubigny is associated with the *plein-air* painters of Barbizon who became the forerunners of Impressionism. He was particularly interested in water and used to paint from a boat which travelled up and down the river Oise.

This drawing of water, wind and vegetation could only have been executed outdoors, possibly from his floating studio. The artist's small sheet of drawing paper seems to hold a vast area of space through which the weather blows freely. The cultivated trees around the tomb stand in marked contrast to the wild, windy nature which surrounds them. Every conceivable twist and turn of the charcoal stick has been employed to describe the dampness of riverbanks, the lightness of air, and the reflections of water. A painted likeness of the dead man could not speak more eloquently of his memory than this.

tombeau de jean jacques rousseau

sir frederick william burton

1816 - 1900

Burton was born in Co. Clare and explored Irish historical and folk themes in his early work. He left Ireland during the famine, however, eventually settling in Britain where he became part of the Rossetti circle. From then on the Pre-Raphaelites influenced his choice of medieval subject matter, with the emphasis on romantic narrative.

The sparcity of tonal work in this drawing bleaches out the features, making it quite different from the detailed patterning of Burton's sumptuous watercolours. Eyes, lips and hair were all emphasised by the Pre-Raphaelites, but this work has much more of a contemporary look than the allegorical muses of Rossetti and Burne-Jones.

Like the façade of a building, La Marchesa's great visage fills the paper from end to end. No bumps of chin or cheek interrupt the flatness of this wide plane, while the eyes are so far apart they are almost on opposite sides of the head and looking in two different directions.

study for la marchesa

pierre-cécile puvis de chavannes

1824 - 1898

Puvis de Chavannes's work was classical in theme but thoroughly modern in technique. The artist's working method can be clearly followed in this crayon drawing. To the right of the figure various try-out poses can be seen; to the left, experiments with mark making are conveniently employed to become the support on which she rests her back. All about the head and arms are clouds of repeated lines and contours. Here we can see where Puvis tried and re-tried a line until he was satisfied with its weight and density.

This frisson of activity lends the whole body of the woman an air of repressed movement. She could almost get up and run, her strong stomach and legs supporting an athletic frame. Like Corot, Puvis de Chavannes falls between art movements, but the individuality of his style impressed many important artists who followed. His use of flat areas of colour and emphasis on dynamic drawing influenced Degas. The simple rhythmic pattern of his compositions can be found in the work of the Nabis and Symbolists. The tall cold figures of Picasso's blue and rose periods show that even he had been looking at this vastly under-estimated maverick of the nineteenth century.

seated female nude

walter frederick osborne

1859 - 1903

Osborne's work alternated between loose Impressionism and accurate naturalism. The two portraits shown here are executed in different techniques but share a similar fleetness of style. Two women from vastly differing age and social groups gaze at us. One became a famous icon, the other may be anonymous.

Maud Gonne is sitting in a chair or standing by an easel in her pinafore. Neither fancy hairdo nor feathery hat overshadow a face that is ordinary, as yet unfrozen in the pose of the great Irish Muse. Though hastily drawn, it is not a hasty drawing. Osborne understood that there was no need to finish the arm and hand of a person whose jawline and dishevelled hair sufficiently expressed a robust character. The blank eyes betray a sadness seldom seen in her official portraits.

The identity of the elderly lady in the pastel drawing *Portrait of a Lady* is unknown. All around the borders of the image are little experimental marks in pastel, as if Osborne were trying out this new medium as he went along. The matriarchal head of this austere lady appears to float in the abstracted background, anchored only by her tender eyes and the extreme whiteness of the bow at her throat.

maud gonne

portrait of a lady

berthe morisot

1841 - 1895

Morisot draws and paints simultaneously, with neither activity taking precedence over the other. This immediacy of response and drawing/painting technique pulls her firmly into a twentieth century sensibility.

The touches of watercolour in *The Sail Boat* are so light that the whole image appears almost as a reflection. The whiteness of paper acts as water surface while objects are indicated with the minimum of marks. Cool colours are used throughout with just a hint of ochre to attract our eyes to the empty boat, bobbing like a bird in the shimmering sunlight. The shaky line drawing adds to the overall effect of buoyancy and impermanence.

The mast of the sail boat breaks the composition in an asymmetrical way, giving a 'snapshot' rather than composed format, and implying the knowledge and influence of photography. Morisot had been a follower of Corot and then Manet and she exhibited regularly with the Impressionists.

the sail boat

giovanni segantini

At first these drawings appear to be imitations of Millet. On closer inspection of their surface composition, however, one can discern the seeds of a future art movement that is more allied to modern times than it is to the nineteenth century.

The use of textured paper, the short flicking strokes of charcoal over the whole surface, the generalised figuration, all are traits reminiscent of the drawings of Seurat who was the leader of Pointillism (or Divisionism) in France.

Giovanni Segantini developed his own form of Divisionism in Italy. He moved away from the solidity and order of sub-Seurat to develop a vision that had overtones of symbolism and fantasy. The spiky, agitated trees and glacial, moonlit setting seen here are forerunners of his later neurotic style. The ghostly figures of his late works have not yet appeared, but may lurk in the enveloping night where the lugubrious heavy-headed sheep are already an uneasy presence.

the shepherd asleep

the return to the sheepfold

49

william rothenstein

1872 - 1945

When I first saw this portrait of Lennox Robinson, only the face and shoulders were visible, the lower 'bad' part of the drawing being hidden by mounting card. Here you see the entire work, including the exact place where Rothenstein's concentration slipped and the drawing of the hand became floppy and disproportionate. This portrait was done in Dublin and donated by the artist himself to the Collection in 1934. I wonder who decided to cover up the mistake?

Lennox Robinson looks every inch the man-about-town in his dinner jacket, his leonine hair swept back from an angular face. Rothenstein was a member of the Bloomsbury set and a socialite on the borders of British bohemianism. He was also a friend of Orpen and a fellow war artist. The certitude of observational drawing is evident here, but so too is the dynamism of strong simple contours influenced by the likes of Degas.

study for a portrait of lennox robinson

alfred stevens

1817 - 1875

This *Head of a Woman* could be mistaken for the work of an earlier century and displays all the signs of an artist who has been studiously copying the old masters. The red chalk favoured by Michelangelo, the anatomical accuracy and detailed light and shade, could almost date this work in the High Renaissance. The linear precision of Holbein can also be cited as an influence.

Stevens was, in fact, a late nineteenth century British sculptor who worked on such public monuments as the Wellington memorial. His studies in red chalk were exhibited at the Royal Academy in 1890.

The beauty of this particular drawing lies in its simplicity and lack of extraneous detail. The volumetric drawing of cheek and shoulder is very clearly the work of someone who understands sculptural space. The helmet of hair or bonnet frames a sullen and mysterious glance. We do not know whether this is a religious, mythological or secular drawing. And therein lies the secret knot of its unravelling.

head of a woman

jean françois millet

1814 - 1875

Millet's subject matter of labourers on the land was politically provocative in the nineteenth century, yet today it has come to represent the most romantic vision of country life. Ironically, prints of *The Angelus* or *The Gleaners* were hung in rural parlours in Ireland and England as sentimental expressions of Christian piety, rather than as any sign of empathy with the toil of French farm workers.

This is one of the earliest drawings by Millet of gleaners collecting chaff. The wavering chalk lines crackle with energy and are concentrated as if by magnet around the central form of women at work. The emptiness of field and sky foregrounds their lonely, endless labour. The double silhouette takes on the awkward shape of a foraging animal.

The second of Millet's works is a nude study accompanied by a long strip of thumbnail sketches. It is a measure of the esteem in which Millet was held by collectors when a strip torn from his sketchbook was so preciously preserved and added to a larger drawing, like a predella panel to an altarpiece.

The large nude lies propped on her elbows in a shady wood. She cannot be construed as mythological as she still wears her kerchief and we can see her discarded clothes amongst the trees. So, although she goes by the very high art title of *The Bather*, it is obvious that she is simply taking a break from work to cool off in the stream. The tiny drawings in the panel above show how Millet struggled to get it right and, as evidence of the artist's own labour, they make a helpful addition to the composition.

studies for *the bather*

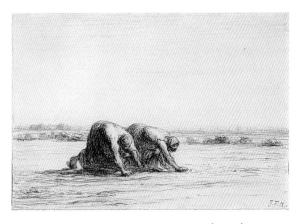

the gleaners

keith henderson

1883 - 1982

Keith Henderson has lived closest to our time, yet his work seems most like the dream of a bygone age. His Darwinian and humanist interests led him to painstaking and faithful illustration of plants and animals. This extraordinary telescopic way of recording nature carries through into his paintings.

The Romaunt of the Rose illustrates a scene from Chaucer. At first glance we read this as Pre-Raphaelite, but closer study reveals the strange world of an encyclopaedic collector of visual facts. Henderson's dry exactitude records every petal and bud, every feather and frond, in this English country garden.

The human beings have to squeeze in to this epic of nature stacked like a deck of cards behind them. They are in danger of being pushed off the shallow wall and right out of the picture plane. Their beautiful tunics and leather belts, their skin and hair, even the buckles of their shoes, are all painted with the same scientific observation that Henderson applies to the surface of a fern.

asleep

the romaunt of the rose

Two particular works from the Collection have provided a special insight for me and a platform for personal response in my drawings. These are *Anima errante* by Paul Klee and *Asleep* by Keith Henderson, two works from the opposing poles of art history. *Anima errante* is the only non-figurative drawing in the Collection and *Asleep* comes from a Pre-Raphaelite inspired, highly figurative tradition.

Sleep was a popular theme with early twentieth century artists and it is no coincidence, of course, that this occurred just as the dreams and inner lives of people were gaining significance through the studies of Freud and Jung.

Keith Henderson's *Asleep* is a world within a world, each chamber opening into another, from the heavy frame to the curtained bed to the body, then the head, then the dream of the girl. It is an image of inwardness that in turn leads us back out into an ever-multiplying space.

Paul Klee developed his own pictorial language around the time of the First World War, influenced by primitive art and the drawings of children. To him art was a language of signs. He realised that when we see an image we immediately invest it with meaning ourselves, that images 'trigger' meaning without our necessarily understanding the shapes we are looking at. In later life Klee studied all kinds of ideographs, hieroglyphics and the mysterious markings in prehistoric caves. *Anima errante* is clearly taken from this period. Klee's incised drawing wanders like the minotaur in the maze of its own making. Paths/lines form and reform themselves around an inner logic that could as easily be vast cosmos as miniature city map.

Klee's following of his own labyrinthine lines through the subconscious seems in total contrast to Henderson's rendered surfaces with their book illustration iciness. Yet it is between the activity of one and subject of the other that an island of common ground emerges. *Anima errante* is the subconscious at work, *Asleep* is an image of that work taking place.

The knot of the subconscious unravels in Klee's earth-coloured scraping just as surely as the dreams of Henderson's girl spill out of her curtained enclosure into the room with us.

My own four drawings come into being on this island between repeated action and awakening image. The giant coils of *Coma Berenices* are seen from a distance clearly as images of entwining hair, while up close they become all-enveloping curtains of line and energy. They are knots of drawing that shift between the gigantic and the miniature, the single and the multiple image. But most of all they are knots of the labour and time, memory and longing that went into their making.

Alice Maher

59

keith henderson

1883 - 1982

asleep

anima errante

coma berenices

alice maher

four drawings
charcoal on paper
1999
each 152 X 183 cms
to the memory of larry maher

index of drawings

Gallery of Modern Art, Dublin pp.100-101 (ill); 1996,
NCAD 250 Drawings 1746-1996, pp. 70-71 (ill)
Lit. N. Gordon Bowe, 'Wilhelmina Geddes', *Irish Arts
Review*, vol. 4, no. 3, p.56 (ill, p.53)
Reg. No. 1766
page 31

Keith Henderson
(b. Scotland 1883 d. South Africa 1982)
The Romaunt of the Rose
Watercolour and pencil on watercolour board,
38 x 42.5 cms
Signed *Keith Henderson* lower right
Prov. J.T. Bennet Poe Bequest, 1910
Exh. 1988, *Critics Choice*, Hugh Lane Municipal
Gallery of Modern Art, Dublin, pp.8-9
Reg. no. 391
page 57

Keith Henderson
(b. Scotland 1883 d. South Africa 1982)
Asleep
Watercolour and pencil on card, 31.5 x 30.9 cms
Signed *Keith Henderson* lower right
Prov. Presented by a friend, no date
Reg. no. 390
page 56 and 60

Augustus Edwin John
(b. Wales 1878 d. Hampshire 1961)
Joseph Hone
Black chalk on wove paper, 45.6 x 35.5 cms
Signed *John* lower right. Inscribed *Joseph Nathaniel
Hone* upper left
Prov. Presented by Mrs John, 1963
Exh. 1965, *W.B Yeats. A Centenary Exhibition*, National
Gallery of Ireland, Dublin (165), p.93
Reg. no. 1218
page 19

Augustus Edwin John
(b. Wales 1878 d. Hampshire 1961)
Study of a Girl (Dorelia with a Scarf)
Pencil on wove paper, 31.6 x 20.6 cms
Signed *John, Paris 1907* lower right
Prov. Lane Bequest, 1913
Reg. no. 162
page 18

Paul Klee
(b. Switzerland 1879 d. Switzerland 1940)
Anima errante
Watercolour and pencil on wove paper, 18 x 27 cms
Inscribed *irrende Seele I / 1934 S2* on backing card
Prov. Bequest of Mr Charles Bewley, 1969

Lit. Yvonne Scott, "Paul Klee's 'Anima errante' in the
Hugh Lane Municipal Gallery, Dublin", *The Burlington
Magazine*, No. 1146. VOL. CXL, September 1998
Reg. no. 1297
page 61

Alphonse Legros
(b. Dijon 1837 d. London 1911)
Study of Two Heads
Silverpoint on laid paper, 24 x 30 cms
Signed *A Legros* lower left
Prov. Presented by Dermod O'Brien P.R.H.A. through
the Friends of the National Collections of Ireland, 1926
Reg. no. 608
page 13

Frederic, Lord Leighton
(b. Scarborough 1830 d. London 1896)
Study of Nude Figure (Juggler)
Charcoal and white chalk on blue paper, 32 x 24.5 cms
Signed *Leighton* lower right
Prov. Presented by Mrs Russell Barrington, 1909
Reg. no. 377
page 27

Sir John Everett Millais
(b. Southampton 1829 d. London 1896)
**Study for an Illustration to Coleridge's
"Love" or Two Figures in a Moonlit Wood
1856-7**
Pencil on wove paper, 13.3 x 10.9 cms
(Pencil drawing on verso)
Unsigned
Prov. Presented by Miss S.C. Purser, H.R.H.A., 1908
Exh. 1908, Municipal Gallery of Modern Art, Dublin
(212), p.42; 1979, *Millais' Drawings*, Arts Council of
Great Britain Touring Exhibition, Bolton Museum and Art
Gallery; Brighton Art Gallery; Graves Art Gallery,
Sheffield; Fitzwilliam Museum, Cambridge and National
Museum of Wales, Cardiff
Reg. no. 375 (a)
page 15

Sir John Everett Millais
(b. Southampton 1829 d. London 1896)
Female Figure
Pencil on wove paper, 16.8 x 12.2 cms
(Pencil drawing on verso)
Unsigned
Prov. Presented by Miss S.C. Purser, H.R.H.A., 1908
Exh. 1908, Municipal Gallery of Modern Art, Dublin
(212), p.42
Reg. no. 375 (d)
page 14

Sir John Everett Millais
(b. Southampton 1829 d. London 1896)
Two Figures on the Ground
Pencil on laid paper, 11.2 x 14.4 cms
Unsigned
Prov. Presented by Miss S.C. Purser, H.R.H.A., 1908
Exh. 1908, Municipal Gallery of Modern Art, Dublin
(212), p.42
Reg. no. 375 (c)
page 15

Jean François Millet
(b. Normandy 1814 d. Barbizon 1875)
The Gleaners c. 1850
Black chalk on wove paper, 14.9 x 21.9 cms
Signed *J.F.M.* lower right
Prov. J. Staats-Forbes Collection. Presented by Sir
William Armstrong, Sir Horace Plunkett, Lord Dunsany
and Mr E.P. Alabaster, 1905
Exh. 1904, Royal Hibernian Academy, Dublin, (303),
p.71 (J. Staats-Forbes Collection); 1905, National
Museum, Dublin (41) p.16, £122; 1908, Municipal
Gallery of Modern Art, Dublin (183), p.38; 1978,
Millet's Gleaners, The Minneapolis Institute of Arts, (2),
pp.16, 40; 1980, *The Peasant in Nineteenth Century
French Painting*, Douglas Hyde Gallery, Dublin (58) (ill);
1993, *Images and Insights*, Hugh Lane Municipal
Gallery of Modern Art, Dublin, pp. 192-193, (ill); 1994,
Development of 19th Century French Art, Ashikaga
Museum of Art; Tokyo Station Gallery; Museum of
Contemporary Art, Sapporo; Daimaru Museum,
Umeda, Japan (11), p.37 (ill)
Lit. P. O'Connor, *Municipal Art Gallery*, 1958, (164) (ill.
pl.6); K. Clark, *Romantic Rebellion*, New York, 1972,
p.294, (ill.226); R.L. Herbert, *Jean-François Millet*,
Grand Palais, Paris, 1975-76, pl.144 and Hayward
Gallery, London, 1976, p.86
Reg. no. 564
page 55

Jean Francois Millet
(b. Normandy 1814 d. Barbizon 1875)
Studies for "The Bather"
(i) 15.8 x 25.2 cms
(ii) 4 x 25.8 cms
Black chalk on thin wove paper
Unsigned
Prov. Lane Bequest 1913
Exh. 1904, Royal Hibernian Academy, Dublin (292),
p.69 (J. Staats-Forbes Collection); 1905, National
Museum, Dublin (48), p.18, £38; 1908, Municipal
Gallery of Modern Art, Dublin (180), p.38; 1994,
Development of 19th Century French Art, Ashikaga
Museum of Art; Tokyo Station Gallery; Museum of

Contemporary Art, Sapporo; Daimaru Museum,
Umeda, Japan (12), p.38 (ill)
Reg. no. 169
page 55

Berthe Morisot
(b. Bourges 1841 d. Paris 1895)
The Sail Boat
Watercolour, black chalk and pencil on paper,
24 x 21.8 cms
Signed *Morisot 47* lower right.
Prov. Presented by the Friends of the National
Collections of Ireland, 1943
Exh. 1926, *Exposition de Berthe Morisot*, Galerie L Dru,
11 rue Montaigne, Paris; 1993, *Images and Insights*,
Hugh Lane Municipal Gallery of Modern Art, Dublin,
p.218-219 (ill); 1994, Friends of the National
Collections of Ireland, *Loan Exhibition of Modern
Continental Paintings*, Dublin, (103); 1994,
Development of 19th Century French Art, Ashikaga
Museum of Art; Tokyo Station Gallery; Museum of
Contemporary Art, Sapporo; Daimaru Museum,
Umeda, Japan (48), p.74 (ill)
Reg. no. 920
page 47

Sir William Orpen
(b. Dublin 1878 d. London 1931)
Hugh Lane Reading
Watercolour, black chalk and pencil on laid paper,
22.7 x 18.1 cms
(Sketch on verso)
Unsigned
Prov. Purchased 1995
Exh. 1978, *William Orpen 1878-1931. A Centenary
Exhibition*, National Gallery of Ireland, Dublin (159)
Reg. no. 1837
page 25

Sir William Orpen
(b. Dublin 1878 d. London 1931)
The Portuguese Woman
Black chalk on wove paper, 42.2 x 32.6 cms
Signed *William Orpen 1904* lower left
Prov. Presented by the artist, 1908
Exh. 1908, Municipal Gallery of Modern Art, Dublin
(203), p.41; 1978, *William Orpen 1878-1931. A
Centenary Exhibition*, National Gallery of Ireland,
Dublin (153), p.68.
Lit. Bruce Arnold, *Orpen. Mirror to an Age*, (ill. p.203)
Reg. no. 321
page 25

Walter Osborne
(b. Dublin 1859 d. Dublin 1903)
Maud Gonne 1895
Pencil on wove paper, 23 x 15.2 cms
Signed *Walter Osborne 1/11/95* upper right
Prov. Presented by Mrs Cecil Armstrong
Exh. 1983-4, *Walter Osborne*, National Gallery of Ireland, Dublin and Ulster Museum Belfast, (86), pp. 148, (ill)
Lit. Jeanne Sheehy, *Walter Osborne*, 1974, no. 432
Reg. no. 379
page 44

Walter Osborne
(b. Dublin 1859 d. Dublin 1903)
Portrait of a Lady
Pastel on wove paper, 39.2 x 31.8 cms
Signed *Walter Osborne* upper right
Prov. Presented by J.B.S. MacIlwaine R.H.A., 1930
Reg. no. 658
page 45

Pierre-Cécile Puvis de Chavannes
(b. Lyons 1824 d. Paris 1898)
Seated Female Nude c.1881
Black chalk on wove paper, 31.7 x 46.2 cms
Signed *P.P.C.* lower right
Prov. Lane Bequest, 1913
Exh. 1908, Municipal Gallery of Modern Art, Dublin (185), p.39; 1989, *Frank O'Meara and his Contemporaries*, Hugh Lane Municipal Gallery of Modern Art, Dublin; Crawford Municipal Gallery, Cork; Ulster Museum, Belfast, (11) (ill) p.50; 1980, *19th Century Drawings and Watercolours*, Hugh Lane Municipal Gallery of Modern Art, Dublin; 1989, Fine Arts Society, Glasgow
Reg. no. 153
page 43

William Rothenstein
(b. Yorkshire 1872 d. Gloucester 1945)
Study for a Portrait of Lennox Robinson
Pencil on wove paper, 41.3 x 36.7 cms
Unsigned. Inscribed *Lennox Robinson* lower right
Prov. Presented by the artist, 1934
Reg. no. 704
page 51

John Singer Sargent
(b. Florence 1856 d. London 1925)
Miss Anstruther-Thomson
Black chalk on wove paper, 34.4 x 23.5 cms
Signed *J.S. Sargent* lower right
Prov. Presented by Miss Annabel Blackburne, 1942
Reg. no. 909
page 17

Giovanni Segantini
(b. Arco, Austrian Trentino 1858 d. Switzerland 1899)
The Return to the Sheepfold 1887
Black chalk and white highlight on wove paper, 32.5 x 46.7 cms
Signed *G. Segantini* lower right. Inscribed on verso *No. 88 en 1887 Rentreé à l'etable crayon conté. G. Segantini Piax + Stamp No. 88*
Prov. Lane Bequest 1913
Exh. 1888, *Italian Exhibition*, London; 1894, *Segantini*, Castello Sforzesco, Milan; 1904, Royal Hibernian Academy, Dublin; 1908, Municipal Gallery of Modern Art, Dublin (182) p.38 (ill); 1978, *Giovanni Segantini*, The Kobe Shimbun, Japan, (D11), p.167, (ill); 1981, *Giovanni Segantini*, Vienna, and Innsbruck, (32), p.88, (ill); 1987, *Segantini*, Palazzo delle Albere, Trento, (80), pp. 178/9 (ill); 1990/91, *Giovanni Segantini 1858-1899*, Kunsthaus, Zurich, (70), p.142, (ill)
Lit. F. Servaes, *Giovanni Segantini: sein Leben und sein Werk*, Vienna, 1902, pp.8, 9-10; M. Montadon (W. Ritter), 'Segantini', *Kunstler Monographien*, no. 72. Bielefeld-Leipzig, 1911; G. Segantini, *Giovanni Segantini*, Zurich, 1949; P. O'Connor, *Municipal Art Gallery*, 1958, (257); T. Fiori, *Archivi del Divisionismo*, Rome, 1969, vol. II, pp. 156, 277; A-P. Quinsac, *Segantini. Catalogo Generale*, Milan 1982, (377), p.260 (ill)
Reg. no. 185
page 49

Giovanni Segantini
(b. Arco, Austrian Trentino 1858 d. Switzerland 1899)
The Shepherd Asleep 1886-8
Black chalk and white highlight on wove paper, 26.6 x 37.5 cms
Signed *Segantini* lower left
Prov. Lane Bequest 1913
Exh. 1904, Royal Hibernian Academy, Dublin (304), p.72 (J. Staats-Forbes Collection); 1905, National Museum, Dublin (53), p.19, £15; 1908, Municipal Gallery of Modern Art, Dublin, (178) p.38; 1978, *Giovanni Segantini*, The Kobe Shimbun, Japan, (D13), p.167, (ill); 1987, *Segantini*, Palazzo delle Albere, Trento, (64), pp. 156-7, (ill); 1990/91, *Giovanni Segantini 1858-1899*, Kunsthaus, Zurich, (54), p.122, (ill)
Reg. no. 186
page 49

Simeon Solomon
(b. London 1840 d. London 1905)
The Acolyte 1873
Watercolour and gouache with glaze on watercolour paper, 23 x 23.3 cms
Signed left *SS 1873*
Label on verso: "No. 11 Simeon Solomon. An Old King and Page. A commission to the artist in 1872 C.A.S."
Prov. Lane Gift 1912
Exh. 1904, Royal Hibernian Academy, Dublin (269), p.65; 1906, *Royal Academy Winter Exhibition*, London; 1908, Municipal Gallery of Modern Art, Dublin (251), p.46
Lit. Simon Reynolds, *The Vision of Simeon Solomon*, pl. 65
Reg. no. 81
page 21

Simeon Solomon
(b. London 1840 d. London 1905)
The Greek Festival 1873
Watercolour and gouache with glaze on watercolour paper on card, 23.2 x 23 cms
Signed *SS 1873* lower right
Label on verso: "No. 12 Simeon Solomon, Greeks Going to a Festival. A commission to the artist in 1872 C.A.S."
Exh. 1904, Royal Hibernian Academy, Dublin (273), p.66; 1906, *Royal Academy Winter Exhibition*, London; 1908, Municipal Gallery of Modern Art, Dublin (250), p.46
Lit. Simon Reynolds, *The Vision of Simeon Solomon*, pl. 64
Prov. Lane Gift 1912
Reg. no. 80
page 21

William Strang
(b. Scotland 1859 d. England 1921)
Study of a Head 1906
Pastel and black chalk on laid watermarked paper, 41.5 x 26cms
Signed *W. Strang 1906* lower right
Presented by the artist c. 1908
Exh. 1908, Municipal Gallery of Modern Art, Dublin (204), p.41
Reg. no. 324
page 37

Alfred Stevens
(b. Blanford 1817 d. London 1875)
Head of a Woman
Pastel on wove paper, 20.2 x 25.9 cms
Unsigned
Pencil drawing on verso
Prov. Gift of Lady Holroyd in memory of her husband Sir Charles Holroyd (no date)
Reg. no. 403
page 53

Patrick Tuohy
(b. Dublin 1894 d. Dublin 1930)
Sean O'Casey 1926
Pencil on wove paper, 46 x 37.8 cms
Signed *Patrick Tuohy 26* lower centre
Prov. Presented by Miss B. Tuohy through the Friends of the National Collections of Ireland, 1937
Exh. 1931, *Memorial Exhibition. Patrick Tuohy R.H.A. Paintings, Drawings, Sketches, 1911-1930*, Mill's Hall, Dublin; 1955, *Portraits of Great Irishmen and Women*, Ulster Museum; 1981, *Willie Pearse Centenary Exhibition*, Pearse Museum, Dublin
Reg. no. 814
page 11

Jack B. Yeats
(b. London 1871 d. Dublin 1957)
An Old Slave c.1911
Pen, ink and watercolour on Reeves black and white board, 26 x 19 cms
Signed *Jack B. Yeats* lower right. Inscribed *An Old Slave* lower centre
Prov. Lane Bequest 1913
Exh. 1913, *Summer Exhibition of Irish Art*, Whitechapel Art Gallery, London (235); 1913, *Aonach na Nodlag*, Rotunda Gardens, Dublin; 1914, *Pictures of Life in the West of Ireland*, Walker Art Gallery, London (38); 1972, *From Yeats to Ballagh*, Konsthall, Lund (44); 1988, *Yeats at the Hugh Lane Municipal Gallery of Modern Art*, Dublin (25)
Lit. Hilary Pyle, *The Different Worlds of Jack B. Yeats. His Cartoons and Illustrations,* (1860), p.256, (Plate no. 16), (ill p.257)
Reg. no. 197
page 29

Jack B. Yeats
(b. London 1871 d. Dublin 1957)
The Travelling Circus 1906
Watercolour and gouache on Whatman watercolour board, 26.9 x 36.8 cms
Signed *Jack B. Yeats* lower right
Prov. Bequest of Miss Josephine Webb, 1924
Exh. 1906, *Sketches of Life in the West of Ireland*, Leinster Hall, Dublin (21); 1945, *National Loan Exhibition*, National College of Art and Design, Dublin (175); 1965, *Loan Exhibition*, Municipal Gallery, Waterford (1); 1972, *From Yeats to Ballagh*, Konsthall, Lund, Sweden (42); 1988, *Yeats at the Hugh Lane Municipal Gallery of Modern Art*, Dublin (24)
Lit. Hilary Pyle, Jack B. Yeats. *His Watercolours, Drawings and Pastels*, (618), p. 152, (ill)
Reg. no. 599
page 29

alice maher

Alice Maher is represented by

The Green on Red Gallery

Dublin tel: 353 1 671 3414

fax: 353 1 672 7117

email: greenred@iol.ie

Solo Exhibitions

1999 **Coma Berenices**, Hugh Lane Municipal Gallery of Modern Art, Dublin

1998 **Le Chemin**, Ecole Vincent Van Gogh, Ville de Mitry-Mory, Paris

1997 **Acre**, Green On Red Galleries, Dublin
Femmes-Fontaines, Le Confort Moderne, Poitiers
l'Arpent (The Long Acre), River Clain, Poitiers

1996 **Swimmers**, Le Credac, Ivry sur Seine, France
familiar, Newlyn Gallery, Penzance
Solo Show, Todd Gallery, London

1995 **familiar**, The Douglas Hyde Gallery, Dublin; The Orchard Gallery, Derry; Crawford Municipal Gallery, Cork
Works on Paper, Green On Red Gallery, Dublin
The Conversation, Belltable Arts Centre, Limerick

1994 **Keep**, Old Museum Arts Centre, Belfast

1991 **Recent Work** Touring Exhibition, Cork, Dublin, Derry, Limerick

1989 **Tryst**, Belltable Arts Centre, Limerick; University College, Cork

1987 **Transfiguration**, On The Wall Gallery, Belfast

Selected Group Exhibitions

1998-99 **Alice Maher & Tim Davies**, Oriel Mostyn Gallery, Llandudno; Edinburgh Art Centre; Triskel Arts Centre, Cork; Ormeau Baths Gallery, Belfast
Lines of Desire - Drawing, Oldham Art Gallery; Bluecoat Gallery, Liverpool; Wrexham Arts Centre, Wales
When Time Began to Rant and Rage, Berkeley Art Museum, California; Walker Art Gallery, Liverpool; Gray Gallery, New York

1998 **The Sky Chair** - A Performance with composer Trevor Knight, Project @ the Mint, Dublin
Terrains Vagues - Between the Local and the Global, Ecole des Beaux Arts, Rouen; Herbert Read Gallery, Canterbury
Temple Bar International Print Show, Dublin
Return to Sender, Hugh Lane Municipal Gallery of Modern Art, Dublin; Telstra Adelaide Festival; Melbourne Next Wave Festival; Darwin Festival; Institute of Modern Art, Brisbane

1997 **Digital Dimensions**, Arthouse, Temple Bar, Dublin
A Century of Irish Painting. Hugh Lane Municipal Gallery of Modern Art, Dublin Hokkaido Museum of Modern Art, Japan; Mitaka City Gallery of Art, Japan; Yamanashi Prefectural Museum of Art, Japan
Redressing Cathleen, McMullen Museum of Art, Boston

1996 **IMMA/Glen Dimplex Awards**, Irish Museum of Modern Art, Dublin
l'Imaginaire Irlandais, École des Beaux Arts, Paris
Tír - Alice Maher and Alanna O'Kelly, Gavle Arts Centre, Sweden

1995-96 **Distant Relations**, Ikon Gallery, Birmingham; Camden Arts Centre, London; Irish Museum of Modern Art, Dublin; Santa Monica Museum, L. A.; Museo Carillo Gils, Mexico City

1995 **Twelve Irish Artists**, Itami Museum, Kyoto, Japan
Art As The Object of Desire, Fenderesky Gallery, Belfast
Compulsive Objects, Rubicon Gallery, Dublin
A-Dress, Winniepeg Art Gallery, Canada

1994 **São Paulo Bienal**, São Paulo, Brazil (representing Ireland)
From Beyond The Pale, Irish Museum of Modern Art, Dublin

Un Pelérinage Kaleidoscopique, Orchard Gallery, Derry; Hugh Lane Municipal Gallery of Modern Art, Dublin; Tyrone Guthrie Centre, Annaghmakerrig; L'Escola de Belles Artes, Lleida; La Rectoria, Barcelona, Le Musée D'Art Moderne, Toulouse

1993 **Relocating History**, Fenderesky Gallery at Queens, Belfast; The Orchard Gallery, Derry
E. V. + A., Limerick City Gallery, Limerick

1991 **Strongholds; New Art From Ireland**, Tate Gallery, Liverpool; The Sara Hilden Museum, Finland

1990 **Irish Art of The Eighties: Sexuality and Gender**, The Douglas Hyde Gallery, Dublin
In A State, Kilmainham Jail, Dublin

1989 **Issues**, Arts Council of Northern Ireland
Art Beyond Barriers, Frauenmuseum, Bonn

1988 **Cotter, Maher, Walsh.** Showntell Gallery, San Francisco
Basquait, Clemente, Coombes, Maher, Wilson, Kerlin Gallery, Dublin

1987 **Alice Maher & Raine Bedsole**, Diego Rivera Gallery, San Francisco

Bibliography

1999 **Knot - Alice Maher draws from the Collection**, Hugh Lane Municipal Gallery of Modern Art, Dublin

1997 **Alice Maher** - Profile 6: Medb Ruane, Gandon Editions, Cork
Ombres - Alice Maher: Green On Red Galleries, Dublin

1996 **L'imaginaire Irlandais**, AFAA, Paris

1995 **familiar**: Fionna Barber / Cécile Bourne, Douglas Hyde Gallery, Dublin, Orchard Gallery, Derry
Distant Relations: Lucy Lippard, Smart Art Press, New York

1994 **22nd São Paulo International Bienal**: Nelson Aguilar, Declan McGonagle

1991 **Recent Work**: Touring Exhibition: Fionna Barber, Triskel Arts Centre, Cork

1991 **Strongholds: New Art From Ireland**: Dr. Penelope Curtis, Tate Gallery Liverpool

1990 **A New Tradition: Irish Art of the 80's**: The Douglas Hyde Gallery

1990 **Alice Maher**: Emer McNamara, Arts Council of N. Ireland

1989 **Art Beyond Barriers**: Marianne Pitzen, Frauemuseum, Bonn

1987 **Irish Women Artists**: Joan Fowler, Douglas Hyde Gallery, Dublin